Nov. 2004

For E

Best wishes,

Kathi Aguero

Daughter of

Daughter of

POEMS by
KATHLEEN AGUERO

Kathleen Aguero

2005 ❖ CEDAR HILL BOOKS ❖ SAN DIEGO, CA

Other books by Kathleen Aguero
> *Thirsty Day* (Alice James Books)
> *The Real Weather* (Hanging Loose Press)

Co-editor, with Marie Harris
> *A Gift of Tongues: Critical Challenges in Contemporary American Poetry* (University of Georgia Press)
> *An Ear to the Ground: An Anthology of Contemporary American Poetry* (University of Georgia Press)

Editor
> *Daily Fare: Essays from the Multicultural Experience* (University of Georgia Press)

Daughter Of
Copyright © 2005 by Kathleen Aguero
All rights reserved
First Edition

ISBN: 1-891812-35-1
Library of Congress Control Number: 2004103377

Cover Design and Typesetting: Kerrie Kemperman
Cover Illustration: "Pomegranate" by Celia Gilbert
Author Photo: Debi Milligan

Distributed by Small Press Distribution
1-800-869-7553
www.spdbooks.org

Cedar Hill Books
San Diego, California 92104
cedarhill_bks@hotmail.com
www.cedarhillbooks.org

For Richard
and for Robert and Veronica

Contents

Acknowledgments

Grateful acknowledgment is made to the editors of the following
publications in which these poems or versions of them first appeared:

Ascent: "Machias Seal Island"
The Birmingham Review: "A Daughter's Nightmare"
Bostonia: "Parable Of Wakening"
The Bridge: "Backfloat"
Calyx: "Selkie" and "Journey with My Sister"
The Chachalaca Review: "After the Visitation"
The Charlotte Poetry Review: "The Swan"
5 a.m.: "Boy/Haircut"
Hanging Loose: "What Has a Child Told You Lately?" and
    "Transformations"
The Harvard Review: "Consultation With A Psychic"
In Posse: "Death Salad"
The U.S. Latino Review: "Climbing Down"
The Larcom Review: "Annunciation," "A Mother's Soup," and "My
    Mother at the Seashore"
The Mystic River Review: "Swim Show"
The Pinyon Review: "St. Joseph on a Roofing Job"
Poetry: "Captain Colette"
Sojourner: "Diana Playing Soccer With Her Nymphs on Cambridge
    Common" and "The Wisdom of Solomon"
Southwest Review: "Exile"
The Texas Review: "Cassandra Mama" and "Medusa"
Words and Images: "Icon"

The author wishes to express her gratitude for the support she has
received from the Elgin/Cox Trust, the Virginia Center for the
Creative Arts, the Scholars Program of the Brandeis University
Women's Studies Research Center, and from Pine Manor College and
those donors to the College who have made possible the Lindsey
Professorship, the Wean Senior Faculty Professorship, the Kellogg
Award, and the Josephine Abercrombie Chair in Writing.

Thanks also to Linda McCarriston, Barbara Helfgott Hyett, and L.R.
Berger for their generosity in helping order and title this manuscript;
to the members of the Monday night poetry workshop: Suzanne
Berger, Erica Funkhouser, Kinereth Gensler, Celia Gilbert, Miriam
Goodman, Helena Minton, Nina Nyhart, and Connie Veenandaal for

their helpful criticism and constant support; to Leslie Lawrence, Denny Bergman, and Elizabeth Galloway for reading portions of this manuscript along the way; to the women writers and friends who organize the house in Duxbury where so many of these poems have been written. Deepest thanks to Richard Hoffman for his careful reading of all my work and for keeping hope alive.

~MIRANDA~

Author's Note:

Based on Shakespeare's play, *The Tempest*, *Miranda* is a series of poems that explores the life of Miranda, daughter of Prospero, after she embarks for Naples to marry Prince Ferdinand.

Prelude

                    The flame
of your father's vengeance leaves you lame
and halting. The aim
of his magic starts to falter.

Raised to mirror
only one, move from that error
to uncover the hidden mother.

The turbulent waters praise
her. The high winds raise
her perfume all around you. Ease

into that small boat, your resolve.

Miranda Recalls Leaving the Island

The ship—a rougher and more populated version
of our island: coils of oily rope,
masts like naked trees with men,
not monkeys, hanging in their branches.
This floating island also filled with noises:
grunting like boar mating from the crew
who pulled the squid-shaped anchor up,
a rush and then a canopy of sails blooming.

The ship's rail cut
my hands, I held so tight. My throat
burned, then suddenly all eyes
were on my father's back and outstretched
arms—red flames and black and finally
white light made me shield my eyes.
My father turned and bowed.
He'd thrown his great book to the sea.
A few days before the tempest
he'd shown me pages blank as clam shells.

The Voyage

Sea merged with sky,
night merged with day
below, all cramped
in one small hold. My father
describing Ferdinand and me
as if we were prize dogs he bred
until I felt flimsy as a spirit
brought here by his command
while Ferdinand grew larger and more taut,
billowed by my father's words.

But whenever I managed to pull myself from Ferdinand,
my father, like some mad puppeteer,
had disappeared. And so I was drawn
back to Ferdinand's orbit—
two stars circling each other, attraction
and repulsion of equal force so we
could not fix onto one another,
nor could we pull away.

Naples

The streets are full of gods.
Some are trees
I fling my arms around,
pressing my face against their solid trunks.
Others, slender with the grace
of herons. Men thick, muscled
like working oxen, or soft
as my milk fed pig, my pet. I want
to touch their thistled beards, tangle
my fingers deep in dark curls. The women,
too, are beautiful and I know even less
of women. I long to see
their breasts unbound and hold
that fullness comparing them to mine,
measure their hips with my hands, breathe
deeply near the hollows of their necks.

Miranda Considers Ferdinand's Vows

He thought his father dead,
his kingdom lost,
and me an angel come to save him.
His heart beat dread, his strength bled,
his arms like ghosts
that could not touch the one who saved him.

When that deadly sun set,
he swore my eyes were the fire he read
life by, my breath the rhythm that saved him.
By daylight we'd promised to wed.

My father appeared to toast
our vows and boast of my bravery
in tempering his ire. Ferdinand
thought me an angel. I craved him.

Miranda Dressed by Her Ladies

Silk chemise lifted over my head.
Home in the sea again.

Corset and pull,
breath beats its wings.

My gown rides the swells.
Stiff foam ruffs my neck.

I'm a bell with no tongue.
Jeweled neck and arms.

Undersleeve, hanging sleeve,
a farthingale to shelve men's hands.

As I rise, teetering
in high chopines, hair knotted tight

with pearls and fresh flowers,
my scalp burns and pinches.

Placed in my palm, a painted fan:

On one side a man in white robes
looks down from a cliff. On the other—I stand,

hair flying back as I hold out my hands,
loose gown blown against me.

Burdensome

He says I nag.
My offer to carry wood for him
was touching on the island,
but in Naples, my insistence to sit at council
and discuss his father's decrees burdens him.
He finds me garish as the bright and fleshy petals
of a tropical bloom here in the black
and burnished ebony of court.

It seems he loves me only when we are alone.

I pace the palace gardens
with a cheetah given me
in honor of my mother, Marianna,
who brought the same pet
from Algiers. Two days ago
I stood in the courtyard to study clouds,
cheetah straining at the leash,
Ferdinand watching me.
He went inside, gave his father
permission to send me away.

Journey to St. Benedict's

Sent like a gown to be refitted,
I watch the palace turrets shrink.
The squeal of carts, the cries of hawkers
give way to bird song and the sift
of branches in the wind. I know
this smell of dung, fruit rotting,
rosemary. We stop to drink
fresh goat's milk in an olive grove.

Inside the Convent

The sisters move, dark shadows flickering
before the image of a tortured man
twisted like Ariel in the tree.
Dominus vobiscum. Et cum spiritu tuo, rhythmic
as the chants which were my lullabies.
I'm taught to kneel before the altar,
and the sorrow I bathe in is light
refracted through a rose-stained window
which opens in the dark chapel
like this heaven the priest speaks of.

The nuns attend this man
in robes as I attended father.

Fallen Angels

On an enchanted island lived a witch
named Sycorax. Her mouth crawled along her face.
Her hair was thorn. Hunched, unclothed,
her great breasts hanging, she sent disaster
on strong winds. Crops failed. Droughts came
where they had never been before.

Those winds that carried hatred
shipwrecked a duke who breathed
into the waters so the very island
nearly drowned. On the seventh day
of battle, he wrapped the land
in harsh white light until the earth scorched
anything that touched it, and Sycorax was blinded.

Caliban showed me the shady grove
where his mother's spirit sleeps.
The ground was moist.
I crept there to rest
in Sycorax's shadow.

Miranda's Dream

Memory and dream—
An image of myself: child before
a great lake at the island's core. In that lake,
a hideous face: one bloodshot eye rolled up.
Long hair, gray but giving off
bright sparks. I thought my heart
would shake my ribcage loose,
my inheld breath explode.

The waters stirred:
soft voices,
the rustling of brocade,
a woman's face, my own,
but sharper.

Nothing more than fear and longing?
The wind slicing, the heat shoving us under its glove?

Then father touched my shoulder, and I woke
on bleached sand, shaded by his cloak.
I'd cried out in my sleep.
He led me to the island's heart.
There was no lake.

Fever

Rain and rain. Small fires
and high plaster walls.
Objects and people so bright
I see through them. Flames.
Music. Breath.
Flight. I mumble
spells. Someone mentions
leeches. I shout "No,"
and call for father.

Scent of thyme and lemon grass.
My breath caught. An old fear
and a new fear. A woman next to me.
The strong line of her jaw.
She opens her mouth and the island's music
rushes over me. Her hand
cool as a stone on my brow.
Familiar sensation of her touch.

Gossip, Rumor

They do not offer prayers here for that woman.

She brought her baby for my blessing.
Look—inside this brooch, Miranda's hair and hers.

She could have had great influence
if with patience she followed the threads
that mark our places.

Monthly we said the old prayers by moonlight,
kept midsummer fires lit.

When his head ached from study,
she rubbed rosemary and ginger
on his brow. She translated charms
from her own language, walked the hills all day
searching for plants he needed.

At night Marianna sang lullabies
from Algiers with birdsong threaded
through them and when the baby woke...

strength and ambition,
but no true sense
of how to move God's will
through worldly channels.

talked to the subjects of Milan without the Duke

no mere abbess could command her

but I'll deny we spoke
and be believed.

She taught the mother whose milk wouldn't come
to brew alfalfa tea, wiped spittle from an aged woman's
    face

      not temper, but a will which would not be stopped.

     She could have had what she wanted,
     but she would not be instructed.

        Athena had no mother,
        why must Miranda?

not for the greater glory of God
but for the animal comfort of it.

How Many Mothers?

Father,

It seems they know
my mother, but speak of her
in whispers. What I hear
confuses me.

How many mothers
did I have?

In Chapel

Just behind the incense—there it is:

rose, warm flesh, stilled water,
decaying leaves beneath.

There's something brushing against
my mind that disappears

when I turn to face it. I am
an invented creature wanting to turn

on the one who made me. This fury
frightens me.

The nuns begin their waking. A kettle
clangs. Someone is drawing water from the well.

But I am held in the mystery of some other day.
I conjure my father's hand on my shoulder as he shows

me a shift in the winds. I'm not moving
into light, not circled safe by darkness.

On First Seeing Ferdinand

I noted his strong back, his legs
whose ankles I measured
with my hands then charting upward
found limbs sinewy and curving,
his hands that stroked my face
more gently than the honeysuckle vines.
Dazed and irritable, I followed him
out of old habit and this new need,
an apt student,
trained in attention and devotion.

Prospero in Trance

This is the time without shadow.
Wrapped in night she leaves.
For her the sun holds back its rising.
She rides. She rides
protected by her fury.
The goatherd wakes, sees only stars.

I shifted the sea
and placed you
in its lap. You've broken free.
You gallop toward me.
Your whole body a demand.

Miranda Sees Prospero Once More

An old man in a white robe,
he knows what he knows.

He gave up his power
in order to save me

and so cannot save me.
Weary, weary,

he swims into words.
If he could shut me like a book

he would. He has a story that dissolves
in his mouth. He shows me the dust in his teeth.

Bluebells and violets.
I slept in his lap.

Ebb tide and waterfall.
I ran by his side.

Fig tree and olive.
I rode on his shoulders.

He can't hoist me up there again.

Prospero's Story

I married a princess of Algiers.
We became twined like fibers in fine thread,
mingled like salt in sea.
But she left my studies for her own.
There were those who said she ruled, not I,
that she conjured devils, had a lover.
By the time we were forced onto a leaking ship,
her belly swelled.

She became another thing I could not rule
and still I loved her though courtiers laughed,
called her virago, witch. But whose child
grew inside her?

By the time we reached the shore,
fresh water couldn't restore her.
She gave birth early, tore her clothes,
her hair like seaweed, slick with sweat.
Every feature on her face so stretched
I told myself it wasn't Marianna
but some sycorax who labored there.
She left me Caliban, your brother.
Half-brother? I felt relief
that day he turned on you.

Prospero's Farewell

Accept this serviceable
life I made you. It has
no magic, but its bread
is what we all survive on.
Return to Ferdinand. Seek
forgiveness. I taught you
spells enough to make him
do your will in little ways.
What else could I have done for you?
Create a suitor out of salt?
Let you live, a crone, to tend
an aging father?

If to the island you must go,
take the magician's robe
to keep you warm.

Sycorax's Daughter

I conjure Caliban, my brother,
crouched within the island's core,
invoke Sycorax, my mother,

relinquish Ferdinand for lover.
Now my heart's both light and sore.
I take Caliban for brother.

Where the anguished spirits hover,
in the great lake's oily maw,
I seek Sycorax, my mother.

Though I still call Prospero father,
I'll not be his learning's whore.
I follow Caliban my brother.

In me split forces fight to mingle.
I may house them if I dare
mirror Sycorax, my mother,

push through one past, view another.
I'll break open Prospero's law,
claim Caliban for brother,
hail Sycorax, my mother.

Arriving

I leave my father's dream,
feeling my way by pain and pleasure
through the landscape, wearing its fragrant,
humid air about my shoulders.
Let the shadow fall from every tree.
Let the night ease from its moon.
Let me bring the sea to my lips,
rinse my hair with brine,
step into the island's mouth,
and sing with it.

Indistinguishable
from cypress, part of rock,
Caliban watches me,
my hands full of shells,
kelp in my hair.
I am here to give him Marianna's face,
Sycorax's secrets. I begin to hum
the song we shared as children.

Mother, Mother, I am singing,
and he answers me,
coming closer, closer.

I am only a little afraid.

~SMOKY RIVER~

Vernal Pool

At the end of winter, a space cleared
and I saw myself reflected
in a vernal pool. All year
I must have been waiting there quietly
while I also went about the noisy
world, keeping appointments,
meeting friends. As silently as I could,
I crept to join myself, but that shy animal
so quickly disappeared
I could have dreamed
this visitation but for the shallow
print left on my mind.

Climbing Down

I didn't want to be left upstairs
with Grandmother, drinking tea
while Father, wrench in hand,
climbed down the stairs with no handrail
into the basement's dark rooms—
taped boxes, saws, nails,
old broken things. *Come away
from that door.* So I cried till he carried
me down in his arms, smell of his skin,
scratchy face, letting me near him,
letting me watch in that mildewed place
where he adjusted hinges, tightened bolts
on his own, while in the warm kitchen
my aunts chopped potatoes, opened
cans from the storeroom below.

When mother called, he handed me back
to be marked by her kisses,
fingertips of flour on my blue shirt.
Then she set me to stirring, safe,
out of his way. I wiped my hands
on my apron as if batter were axle grease.
I would command the pipes
that kept the house running.
I would control the furnace below.

Sister/Legend

Would you go down to the smoky river for her?
Back through the quaking tunnel,
into the slick cave? Would you sing
all the while, *Sister, I'm coming*?
She holds your history in her bones.
Like her or not, she waits
at the end of the same cord.
She's all you won't dare and you promised
to be home for her. But already
she's making a slow turn,
growing toward another sun. Maybe
you looked before she was ready.
Now you can't take it back.

Or maybe you rescue her:
she drifts through the rooms
of your days, arctic hands, face
blank as a sidewalk, or grabs
you, hissing snakes in her hair,
their tongues in your face.
Something you shared at birth
she swallowed whole. Who's to say
you're the brave one?
Who's to say who's been saved?

Journey with My Sister

Naked, except for our waterproof backpacks
we swam the winding river. At noon
we'd climb onto the bank and drip,
spread a blanket, picnic. Our flesh
puckered, our long hair tangled
like the roots of water lilies. By mid-month
we moved awkwardly on land.
One night my sister confessed
her true objective: to move backward
into water. She enticed me with the weightlessness,
the huge expanse of our sea life.
By the time we reached the ocean,
her metamorphosis, at least, was complete.
She celebrated in her new voice while,
envious, I waved and clutched the pack she no longer needed,
watched her smooth gray back speeding
like a ribbon from the shore.

Persephone, Returned

One by one, the things I'd brought from home
all disappeared. My pastel dresses too ingénue,
he said, and bought me more in slinky
black and silver. My teenage charm bracelet—
sentimental, replaced with heavy sapphire,
jet. He dressed me, chose my makeup,
did my hair, but when he took my locket—
Not that, I said. He laughed. His look
was steel against my throat. One step toward me
and I understood I had no friends.
The second time, he grabbed
my upper arm and left a mark.

In spring when I'm let home to visit—
daisies blooming everywhere.
My mother's overjoyed to see me.
We roam the fields, our arms around
each other's waists, the way we used to do.
*I like to see the roses in your cheeks
again,* she says. I catch her covert glance:
She doesn't like the bruised look
of my eyes, my hollowed face.
She offers apricots the color of sunset,
tomatoes bursting with juice,
oranges, berries, my favorites. *I rarely
get fresh fruit,* I say. She doesn't
answer.

At the end of summer, he sends for me—
a sleek black limousine, a diamond brooch
to match my tears. *You don't want
for a thing,* my mother always says
looking at these gifts, then pointing
to the fields already parched,

the rest unspoken. Each time,
despite myself, she has to peel my arms
from off her shoulders. *Every woman knows
some hardship.* She hands me over
to my husband's driver.

        Of course,
I was flattered when he noticed
me, a local girl. He was urbane, handsome,
wealthier than any man I'd met. I mistook
his appraisal for praise. One moment
I was fainting in his arms, the next
packed up beside him in that car. My mother
waving from the yard. My father,
in the parlor toasting himself with champagne.

The rooms in this vast house
are dark and quiet. Men sipping
fine brandy, sleek women trailing
perfumed scarves, drift in and out. The house is
strangely empty in the day. He sleeps one heavy leg
across me. When I stir to see the morning sun
Don't go, he says, and it is not a plea.

We understand each other now,
he murmurs, his large hand in the hollow
of my back as he steers me through
the room greeting guests at smoky parties.
I see myself from far away. *Those aren't what you want,*
he says tonight when I choose common daisies
for my hair. I let them drop, the sharp
heels of my shoes crushing them. My own body,
cold to my touch. My face,
a still life in the mirror.

Medusa

She surfaced from Poseidon's rape alone
but for Athena plaiting snakes into her hair.
Who wouldn't want a face that turns a man to stone?

The most beautiful of three sisters turned
Gorgon, yet feeling human pain, there
in the temple where she fought alone.

Out of pride Perseus brought her snake head home,
wedding present for an exiled mother who, in despair,
needed a face to turn her consort into stone.

Think how the Trojan women moaned,
resisted being herded onto nightmare
ships, ravaged by Greeks. Not alone,

their children watching, plotting to be grown
to warriors or stunned by terror of what they'd share
unless they found a face to turn men into stone.

Think of any woman caught in war, in mundane
violence, atoning for her body's flesh and bone
praying only she might wake alone.
Why wouldn't she want a face to turn men into stone?

A Mother's Soup

Who knows what floats in a mother's soup?
Though I try to reassure my daughter,
who is carefully examining then spooning
anything solid onto her bread plate,
she doesn't trust me. She prefers food
that comes in plastic wrappers or is knocked
out of a can. Is that parsley or a flake of dry skin?
Some part of the animal she doesn't like to think of
boiled unrecognizably? This soup is a murky pond
with a soft bottom, a place where eels wrap themselves
around her legs, where the corpses of small crabs are
   tossed
down the front of her bathing suit by every wave.
Womanhood is contagious. Did her mother spit in the
   soup?

Cassandra Mama

Don't forget your jacket. You'll catch cold.
Stay on well-lit streets. Drink your juice.
No, not by yourself. You've been told
before. A mother's voice rattles, loose

change in her children's ears.
As their responses become cryptic, she gets verbose,
frantic that they listen, her fears
growing as their silence comes in larger doses.

Still, she's at it all the time.
Now they're leaving notes like *Gone. Back
later.* No where. No when. She mimes
composure as they give her flak

for nagging. *Get a life. Don't worry.*
She imagines strangers lurk in wooden horses,
sees fires mount the walls. A scurry
of knives in the night. She counts losses

before they happen. No matter what
she says, she knows they will not heed
her. No matter that she knows, she can't not
tell it. No matter, what they need

is to ignore her. She won't say
what she really fears—You're mortal.
They're on Olympus, far away—
and she's buzzing at the portal.

To Bossy Girls

Some of us, you'd never guess we had such
bossy pasts. I have a friend who made her
friends be monkeys while she played Sheena, rushed
around the jungle giving orders.
I used to form these clubs—you're in/you're not—
and at a conference got grown men to eat
with hands behind their backs. The pie was hot,
stuck in their beards. I marveled—what sheep!
After that, such power seemed too easy,
trivial. Twenty then, I made a vow
to try to be a sweeter me.
Likewise, my "Sheena" friend gave up her crown.
But let some skinny girl assert her will,
we cheer her victory; we want it still.

Diana Playing Soccer With Her Nymphs on Cambridge Common

Our Lady of the Wild Things is pent up in the goal.
Unadorned, hair bound in braids,
her nymphs protect her honor. She's too aloof
to beg like lesser girls, but when the coach calls
for substitutions, she looks arrows his way. Sprung,
she sprints to offense, nymphs whooping at her side.
Out of youngest childhood, they're not ball shy.
They throw their changing bodies with abandon,
crashing into one other, checking
with their just-formed hips.
A player from the other team falls down,
tripped by her untied lace. Someone kicks
the ball from her, skimming her knee,
and boots it to Diana, who crazed
after her long time in the goal, can barely control
her foot work. Still, she angles
the ball up field, weaving through the opposition. Score!
High fives and sweaty hugs. They keep the ball
up there so long their own defense is dancing
hip-hop out of boredom, the new goalie
calling to their coach, *Daddy, get me out of here!*
Players on the sidelines wild
to go back in. You can see why Venus has nothing
to offer these girls, why they don't even
notice passing men glance curiously
their way. Their fathers' faces glow,
beguiled by their eleven-year-old daughters.
Their mothers' smiles, more shadowed,
would like to keep them there forever—
safe and vibrant. Shoppers come more thickly
on the footpath now, and farther down a truck arrives
with lunch for the homeless. The older team gathers
to play next, boyfriends at their sides, but these girls

have two more minutes and they're in the game.
Afterwards, the teams debrief then mingle.
Arms around each other, they gossip about school
until their parents' calls grow more insistent
and one by one they leave the sacred grove.

A Daughter's Nightmare

You think you know everything
about your mother. I remember that.
You know her smell. You wear
its perfume on your pulse. Then,
someone tells you about the secret
adult life, puzzling, a little
disgusting, and you sense there may
be a time when your mother forgets you.
If you could find the door
to the room that holds her then,
would you open it
or would you be too afraid?

After her nightmare,
my daughter climbs the stairs to our room
and stands in the doorway
until I call her twice from the bed.
Then she curls
into her mother, her knees
poking my belly, her breath
veiling my face.

Pajama Day at the Daycare Center

My daughter sleeps in her "wedding gown"
so she can call it pajamas and wear it to school
with her Big Bird slippers the next day.
For once we don't argue about clothes.
In the classroom it's like Christmas Eve,
only better. The children wear nightgowns with frilled hems,
fuzzy Dr. Denton's with blue stars;
one even wears a red nightcap.
Our eyes blur like windows in the rain. But the children
walk right past us to fetch scissors and paper,
as if no one's hand was stroking their soft hair.
In her long white dress, my daughter's lost in painting as
   in sleep.
When I say good-bye she doesn't look up.

Puella

You gird your perfect body every day
to do fierce battle with the world. You don
your headphones, sneakers, jeans, practice your voice
and gestures for the fray. You cross the street,
ignoring catcalls, whistles, as you dodge
the cars and buses in your way. And I,
in my armor of scars, take fright and urge retreat.
Intent in combat, you can't hear my cries.
Again, again, you charge—eyes straight ahead,
mouth set, hair gelled to a stiff helmet;
you ride a reckless, blindered horse.

Baltimore Catechism

Why must we suffer?
We do it in the name of Christ.
So that when our time comes,
we'll be brave soldiers of the Lord.
          (When my mother makes my lunch,
             I ask for something small
             because when you eat your lunch
             you're not allowed to talk.
             You have to eat it fast
             and you have to eat it all.)

How do we sin?
We sin in thought and deed.
          (We sin while we're asleep.
             We're sinning while we breathe.
             I'm sinning while I sit here
             and Sister catches me.)

Of what must we beware?
Of the seven deadly sins.
          (If you don't know your letters
             that's because of sloth.
             I know all my letters,
             but thinking that is pride.)

Sister reads a story:
A girl fell down the stairs.
Her guardian angel pushed
her because she told a lie.

Why are we bad?
We were born in original sin.
          (Who isn't here?
             My mother isn't here.

I must be very bad
or she wouldn't have left me here.)

What is extreme unction?
The last sacrament of God.
Right before you die, the priest blesses
the instruments of sin.
He makes crosses on your hands,
your ears, your eyes, your mouth, your nose.
        (Crosses on your nose? Even on your nose.)

It's time to leave the building.
We keep our mouths pressed shut,
eyes front, arms stiff.
We march.

Impossible Mary

In sixth grade we all want to wear the white dress that makes us the one to place the crown on Mary's head on May Day. That's the closest thing to being Mary—eternal virgin, never tempted, never tempting, not like us, eleven years old and already the priest teaches *Wear your clothes tight enough to show you're a woman, but loose enough to show you're a lady.* We can see this is going to be tough as Sister runs her hand over our legs to make sure they're covered by nylons not bare and an incitement to sin in others which sticks to us like *I'm rubber, you're glue.*

After Sister gives the long white dress to quiet Elizabeth, straight "A" student whose mother gives the nuns rides wherever they want to go, the rest of us fight over the four pastel dresses that will mark us as handmaids of Mary. The rule is, like Cinderella's shoe, if a dress fits, you wear it. We suck in our stomachs, we pouf out our busts, those invitations to sin, trying to fill the form of goodness.

And is it fair that Carol Mulligan who wears lipstick after school should get one? Or Margaret who goes in the woods with boys? So many good girls in shapeless navy jumpers left to sing in the chorus *Oh Mary, we crown you with blossoms today* while behind them boys whisper about the size of their breasts or pull on the backs of their bras. So we girls in the chorus are angry and envious—another sin. Until our whole world becomes one long occasion of sin we can only avoid by abandoning our bodies before they grow up or fasting them into submission as the martyrs did. Most of the female saints we know died to save their virginity—we don't even know where ours is. How can we pray to Jesus, a boy, for guidance in this situation? Mary's our only hope.

For Bridget Who Wants to Be a Priest

This sacrament won't bless
you. God doesn't make it
to the girl child. What you always feared—
not enough love to go around.
                          You're on your own.
You set off with a bundle on a stick,
stepping hopefully off the edge. If your nerve fails,
nothing is solid and the worst part
is knowing that.

                    Or look at it another way:
Your brother's ordained. With him
the bloodline ends. All that
on his shoulders, while you skip away,
free woman at last, so light
without the drag of God's eyes
that you float straight to heaven,
right through those gates,
while your brother, draped in the heavy blanket
of love, the keys of the kingdom making
him stoop, is stuck forever
in the fields of the Lord, jostled
by sheep.

Winter Burial

The guinea pig frozen in a plastic bag,
we chip at the unyielding earth. The shoebox
not buried deep enough. I fear
he will resurface in spring. His shroud
not biodegradable. And my daughter's note
buried with him: *You had a hard life G.P.*
I didn't take good care of you, but I loved you.
Already she has become a mother.

Hard Labor

On the clock there was night,
there was day, but for me there was nothing
but one long, hard moment,
a gargantuan pressing and pushing
like squeezing water from a stone,
and I was the stone and you
would not be water.

I was in a long tunnel
wanting to crawl back nine months
but I couldn't get out the way
I got in, so I held to that
stubborn knot at my center.

Touch the head. See the crowning,
and they brought me a mirror,
but the thought made me sick,
so I snatched back my hands
and averted my eyes. Couldn't they see
I was held by the thinnest of threads
and I wouldn't let go?

I shrieked at the midwife
as you came free
scrabbling from my belly to breast,
drenched in the scent of my own smoky blood.
While the nurses gossiped and stitched,
you fed. I was dazed. I was emptied,
discarded by pain.

Red Piano

My son wakes and asks me
for his little red piano,
only he can't think of the word *piano*
so he mimes playing one.
I say he never had a toy piano,
but he insists I put it
with his blocks beneath the crib.
When he looks and doesn't find
it there, he glares at me
all morning.

I want to tell him I've also suffered
such confusion. Once balding men came
to cut down the raspberry bushes
I thought of as mine. They were dressed
like clowns in baggy suits and ruffs.
This was one of my earliest memories.
Later I called it a dream.

Boy/Haircut

This time he doesn't want
to play with the maze of wooden beads
you push along thick wire. This time
he studies the book of hairdos
choosing several styles—all
short on the sides, straight up
on top. None of the models
sports thick, restless curls,
cheeks full as pillows.
Still, the hairdresser does her best
cutting then glancing down
to check the photo while he sits
somber, only his head poking
out from white towels.

When she lifts his chin to the mirror,
he can't stop his smile.
His mother sees a man with a five o'clock shadow,
cheekbones that could bruise you,
hair that would cut your hand.

Backfloat

My son practices the weightlessness
of astronauts and calls me in to see.
His four-year-old body, stretching
the length of the tub, floats
about an inch above its cold, green bottom.
Blond curls swirl, a snaky halo,
and the water's oval frame just skirts
his eyes and mouth. His eyelids close.
So white, so still, so slack, as if he's sealed
back in himself. His ears fill.
He smiles but won't respond
when I call sharply, *That's enough.*
Sit up! Sit up!

What Has a Child Told You Lately?

Recently my daughter told me no,
that I'm wrong, people do die
from doing naughty things;
dead mosquitoes will
come back to life
if you take them outside
and let their mouths fill with air;
that I'm not the boss of her,
that she can shout at me if she wants
and I can't leave
because we're both
in the car and I'm
driving.

Swim Show

We're seated in the bleachers just above
the pool. My son works on his crawl.
He's mastering the element I love.

The coach blows the whistle and another
boy dives in. My son reaches the wall,
does a flip turn. From above

I imagine the silky cover
of water on his skin, the slick haul
of the body through an element elastic as love

at its best. Hard not to think of
womb, fluid, cave, deep pull
from my body. Again I'm above

looking down as he moves
toward air. The water behind him heals
from the sharp kick of mastery. I love

his new muscled body though it shoves
us apart. Now he waves, calls,
mugs for his family above
as he towels off the body I want him to love.

The Swan

My mother brings the swan home like a moon
in her arms. She has no idea of its power,
has never heard the story of the angry swan
who broke a window with its wings.
How beautiful, she says and reaches
toward it as if toward glowing glass
which will not burn her, while I glower,
always the fearful child at the top of the hill
clutching my sled while she speeds
down the icy surface laughing.

The swan settles like water
into its basket as my mother
strokes the snowy feathers
the way she tries to stroke
my hair until she hits
a tangle and I jerk away.
Come here, she motions, *feel how soft.*
Both of them look up at me,
heads cocked. Slowly I move
forward, extend my arm
toward the body of the swan which rears
and hisses until my mother
soothes it, bending
her graceful head close to the bird's,
her long hair a shield
of feathers around her face.

Mother at the Seashore

Beneath the sun that makes us near transparent,
I see your hair white,
your skin grown paler, too,
the edges of your body fading first.

The children snake around
my legs. Each time I approach you,
Mother, I'm anchored
to their need.

You turn your face from me
at last: a mother tethered
to her daughter until the knot
grows slack and leaves a daughter
tethered to her children in return.

I'm not the heart's ease
you thought you had stored up.
You study seaweed tangling
the ocean floor. Now I'm the one
to let you go
into the stirring waters.

~VIGIL~

Captain Colette

Upon the Captain's death his family found: "Two hundred, three hundred, one hundred and fifty pages to a volume; beautiful cream laid paper or thick 'foolscap' carefully trimmed, hundreds and hundreds of blank pages. Imaginary works, the mirage of a writer's career."

Earthly Paradise, Colette

In the heat of the day I withdraw
to blotter, inkstand, foolscap.
I wrench my mind to find a match
for the green of the walnut in our garden,
for the call of the blackbird in its branches.
To give pulse to—not just recount—
stories of the heart,
the subtlety of family ties
that elevates our daily life to godliness
or finds its image magnified in tragedy.
It takes a thousand words to mark one moment's passion.
When I think of Racine, the master,
my own heart soars then chokes.

I put away my pen,
exhausted.
The purest language is possibility.
The blank page contains it.

Machias Seal Island

Try not to point. Don't move,
the Captain says,
and brings the dinghy closer to the shore
where auks nest. Puffins bob beside us
or fly like little wind-up toys,
wings working hard.

The seal skins the monkfish alive
as if peeling off a surgical glove,
then dives for it again,
diving and biting,
till nothing is left but the head—
and then that's gone.

What is it that I've brought my children here to find?
The creatures with whom we share the world?
Or for what I'd name *silence, solitude,*
though the air is loud with cries,
rocks thick with life?
Because we have no God

before whom to feel small,
perhaps I bring them here.
The absence of the human is the closest
I can come to understanding
what will empty me,
vast gray horizon broken by one rocky island.

Selkie

When I first came to land
I thought I cried the salt out like a sea turtle,

but my husband licks it
from my breasts each night.

Landlocked childbirth confused me. After that,
he wouldn't let me go. My muscles sensed

the sealskin bunched in some dark place.
I searched and searched.

In spring and autumn
when he oils it, my human skin

grows soft and full. At night I wake
alone and feel the swelling, but as I rise

to catch him at it, I hear the latch,
his shadow in the doorway.

What is this love that let him
take me like an oyster from its bed?

I bore five children that split
me like a hook. I love them,

but they anchor me to shore.
At dusk I walk to the farthest rock.

Surrounded by water, I sit and hear
my sisters call. I see the sleek forms

of my sea children diving into waves,

pulling me to them like a tide. I want

the animal ocean, gray flanks
heaving liquid as a snake, solid

as silk parting the air. The muscles
in my back and stomach arching

for a dive. The salt is in my mouth now.
I long to sing again, but my own voice frightens me.

At the Zoo

Just as we're about to leave
the tiger wakes. His roar
echoes inside the enclosure
then he appears: his tongue
a wet slab of pink passing
over his teeth and lips;
his open mouth a black moon.
He lifts his tail and a great yellow stream
splatters the wall. *Look at his penis
and balls!* my son shouts. Already
we have forgotten the seals, dark muscle
in the water; the sad orangutans
scratching their old men's bellies, even
the giant polar bear who circles
the edge of the pool. Orange, black, white,
the tiger's stripes rise and set
as he hunkers past, his bulk
the horizon that fills our eyes.

Fitcher's Bird

I sit close to my mother. I ask her
to read it over and over, "Fitcher's Bird."

Even Mama says it's good to share,
but when the oldest daughter
gives the beggar bread,
he touches her, and, just like that,
she's in his basket. At first,
he's nice. When he leaves
to do his sorcery, he gives her keys
and an egg to carry. Every room
in his house is full of presents
till she gets to the third door.
Once she goes through that door,
she has to keep the secret—
cut up bodies and an axe.
Each sister tries, but blood
on the egg gives it away.

       I want to be
like the last sister, brave and smart enough
not to get caught. But even here,
close to my mother, I don't feel
brave or smart. In bed,
when I'm afraid, I go right to the part
where she makes herself a bird.

Transformations

Now I am ready to tell how bodies
change into different bodies—Ovid

Jawbone moving like a glacier toward its surface.
Smooth cheek growing rough.

A small swell of hip, a tiny push beneath the T-shirt.

Meanwhile, something vaguely familiar looks back from
    your mirror,
something about the eyes, the mouth—your mother's face
now focused in your glass. You notice your daughter
wearing your former features though you don't remember
losing them or giving them away.

Surely you should feel a change like this—
the weight of your cheeks as they droop toward your chin,
your throat slackening.

The rest of your body, as you look down on it,
is out of kilter, too. Your weight unchanged,
but your clothes strain in new places.
You lend them to your daughter for play.
She fits right into them and claims them for her own.
You remember all the elegant dresses you borrowed
from your own mother's closet and how,
after you had modeled them, she didn't want them back.

How does the household function so predictably
amidst the body's constant changing?

The children become gods and giants.
You metamorphose into a small bird, a shrub.

Parable of Wakening

He is the first thing she sees
so she thinks he is the sun.

She is the first thing he's wakened
so he thinks he is a god.

She mistakes his strangeness for brilliance,
her gratitude for love.

He mistakes her beauty for serenity,
her desire for compliance.

But as her hunger grows,

he leaves to shoot birds
whose soft fall to the ground

remind him of his lover
falling backward into sleep.

The moment of each death
is like the moment of her wakening.

Consultation with a Psychic at Forty-One

I'm longing to hear
that fascinating narrative—
my life.

Firm cheeked and manicured,
contact lenses and a business suit,
the psychic closes her eyes and inhales:

Your husband loves you.
Your children are comical. In the summer,
you'll take a short trip. You'll keep
the same job for three years.

I'm still deep breathing, but she's opened her eyes
and seems pleased to have given me
a becalmed mid-life.
I'm stunned. She thinks it's enough.

Narcissus and the Movies

Poor love, we expect it
to lift us out of the ordinary, an ordinary
expectation after all, only satisfied
in the movies by the camera's adoration.
So why do we mock Narcissus?

He was only sixteen, lonely, feeling
unlovable, not yet grown into those
gorgeous looks. Restless, he'd rise
every morning, oil his bow. He didn't
care if he shot anything. He raced
through the woods trying
to silence his own steps. When his legs
began to wobble, he'd throw
himself down, pressing into the earth
that cooled his skin, drinking
the good smell of sweat and decay.
His companions confused him, sidling up
to him, stroking his arm. What did they want?
He wanted someone who knew what he meant
when he had trouble saying it. Someone
who wouldn't grow impatient as he fumbled
to express all he felt. Someone—
like himself. Those nymphs flirting around,
pouting, posing, were they making fun of him?

Then he came to the water . . .
Remember, he'd never seen that flawless face before.
Looking in that pool was like watching a movie
in which the actor, the person who wakes
with clumped hair and sour breath, falls away,
and the actual star, freed from his mortal
medium, slowly turns from the camera
to find himself in you. Inside Narcissus

something broke and blossomed.
How patiently the beloved waited
for him to speak. How seamlessly the other
understood, agreed. Echo nattered on
wanting the last word. For once
he hardly heard her. Finally
peaceful, finally whole, accepted
reflected. Who wouldn't fall in love?

                You can't keep
that feeling with you, we older lovers know.
In real time, real light, your lover will have
irritating habits, interrupt or read the newspaper
while you speak and neither of you will be
so beautiful as movie stars. Disappointed,
we name a poisonous bulb for Narcissus,
who, in the rawness of his adolescence,
forgot to hold anything back.

Grandparents

They stand outside their home in Florida.
Retired now, they squint into the sun.
Surprised to find how much I look like her,
I study them for hints of what's to come
but see nothing. In this photo they're fit
and smiling, arms linked. Alice and Al—
their ordered house in which he couldn't sit
for very long, his restlessness a jail
in which he strained while she, good wife, crocheted
and tended plants. Now, traveling through her lungs
a restless cancer grows. Would she have stayed
in New York had she known? He's not yet stunned
by loss. Someday he'll put a trigger to his head,
but now there's cactus, sun, card games ahead.

But now there's cactus, sun, card games ahead;
her chunky jewelry, his Hawaiian shirt.
Beyond I see how one street always led
straight to another, lawns that showed more dirt
than grass. No trees and something stark—
white bungalow, an iffy dream. They look
so posed, like dolls propped up before a stock
backdrop. One son had visited. He took
this photo that doesn't show me anything
I need to know. But she is standing close
to her four sisters in another, holding
a baby in her arms. Its christening robe
falls almost to her knees. She beams with pride.
Al took the shot or paced off to one side.

He took the shot or paced off to one side.
When, later, he couldn't pace, what did he think?
When he got ill? He took his fears for drives
in his big car. When we were young, he'd wink

and call us *monkeys.* Nothing grim in our
grandpa. He had a gun he'd show to the
police if he ever got stopped for minor
traffic violations. They'd call him *sir*
and didn't seem to mind. We were in back.
Pretend to be asleep, my brother said,
and so we did. One day the crack
of gunshot would be heard as sky turned red
with dawn. But then we swam in inner tubes
just off his boat. He tossed us sugar cubes.

Just off his boat, he tossed us sugar cubes,
as Nana served her special deviled eggs
on those excursions aboard the *Jackie II*
named for my brother. Sometimes I'd beg
to have a boat named after me, to know
girls could be sailors, too. He wasn't annoyed
by bleached streaks in my teenaged hair although
he'd kept a tight rein on his wife and boys.
He mellowed as he aged, or so we thought.
He let my Catholic mother through his door
once she stood up to him. He always bought
us gum—Wrigley's Doublemint. He'd snore
after meals, napping in this very chair
I write in now, its slipcover threadbare.

I keep it though, springs shot, cover threadbare,
and sometimes think of him—Thanksgiving at
their house, taking his nap, the living room where
the men gathered for a smoke, relaxing
while the women cleared and cleaned. That done, we'd
    bathe
in Nana's recessed tub, our sudsy curls
like whipped cream on our heads. (That photo saved
inside the family book.) I never learned
exactly what he did—in charge of some
big building, mother said—or why he didn't

like Catholics. Did he run away from home
to join the cavalry? I thought he'd ridden
with Rough Riders up that hill. I'd get
confused about the dates. I'm not straight yet.

Confused about the dates, I'm not straight yet
if when he came back home he really found
his parents had moved, then, at the store, met
his mother buying bread. Such tales sound
half made-up. Perhaps they are. A family
needs some mystery to lift it above
the ordinary life. Another homely
tale—my father, premature, inside the stove,
his grandma says, *to keep him warm,*
Alice. But better he should never have been born.
I used to marvel that he wasn't harmed.
What if they'd turned the heat too high? Forlorn
and cooked. About my grandpa, here's another yarn—
his father came from Cuba to sell guns.

His father came from Cuba to sell guns—
Does that explain the way he'd end his life?
Too pat. When Nana died he came undone—
productively. He'd been strict when his wife
had been alive: no drinking in the house.
He liked to keep her to himself, though she
had friends (and all those sisters), coffee hours.
He'd been burdened by possessiveness. Freed,
he'd go to parties, have a drink, leaving
before too long. Afraid when he got ill
of hospitals, of staying still. Breathing
at seven when friends found him. Had his strong will
pushed for life or death? At barely dawn, they heard
the shot outside his house in Florida.

The Story of Story

The delicacy of story
the democracy of story
the coyness of story
the lifeboat of story
the old shoe of story
the corset of story
the tight pinch of story
the salt and pepper of story
the soft sigh of story
the midnight of story
the ice age of story
the high tide of story
the menses of story
the egg of a story, the pit
the meat and potatoes story
the Beaujolais, Chardonnay, Guinness of story
the rot gut of story
the pabulum of story
the domestication of story
the closet of story
the dumpster of story
the divorce of story
the crash of story
the intravenous of story
the drop dead of story
the mummification of story
the burial of story
the end of story

THE RESURRECTION OF STORY!

the deification of story
the reification of story
the green leaves of story

the warm flesh of story
the tight ass of story
the high heels of story
the lipstick of story
the fur of story
the long tongue of story
the penis and vulva of story
the sexing of story
the sharp teeth of story
the yellow toenails of story
the smooth breast of story
the one eye of story
the feces of story, the urine
the sour breath of story
the pain of story
the good guts of story, eviscerated

the crumpled frame of story
the eight wheels of story
the appetite of story, its rapaciousness
the volcano of story
the eruption of story, the flood
the arson of story
the felony of story
the judgment of story in the court of story
the shame of story
the imprisonment of story
the release of story

the ejaculation of story
the peep show of story
the cartwheels of story
the brass band of story
the anthem of story
the four stars of story
the weapons of story
the bombing of story

the ashes of story
the snowfall of story
the blossoming of story
the bird-song, wind-sift, slow fall of story
the insomnia of story
the somnambulism of story
the guest of story
the alarm of story
the assassination of story
story as hunter, story as prey
the door of story—the open and shut of it
the howl of story
the wound of story
the whimper of story
the surgery of story
the suicide of story

story on holiday in Paris or at the beach
the sunburn of story
the banquet of story
the bankruptcy of story
the passion of story
the cooling of story
the cooking of story
the serving of story
story consumed
story spit out
the discipline of story
the cult of story
the saga of story, its many lives

Before and After

Giddy, Queen of the May,
tipsy with unfocused possibility,
now I'm in a Twelve Step program.
Sober, I walk the line gravity draws.
But no, you're no cold rainfall,
more a steady sun, a solid plot
that grows when tended, invites me
to tend, then tends me tenderly.
So that's how it is. The rootless one
takes root and sometimes feels confined.
The planted one grows restless.
What is love if not this steady echo,
systole, diastole? The way salt
mimics sugar, or water rests on oil.

Icon

In this photograph, you rise from the summer garden as if you grew there. Leafy branches in the background frame your torso; flowers in front blend with the larger flowers on your blue kimono which flows down your shoulders like water. Your eyes squinting slightly against the sun, the copper flame of your hair, and your smile as fixed as a billboard image dwarf the woman you became: the woman who smoked incessantly and stubbed her butts out on the wooden table, who forgot to wash, who was afraid to walk to the mailbox, whose anxious breath came sobbing out, who wrote herself notes of encouragement, nearly illegible, on scraps of paper mixed with the cigarette ashes and butts, who fed her cats but not herself, who hoarded anti-freeze and pills and one day took them.

The woman in the photograph is smiling you out of existence, out of our memories and we love her. Now it's she we mourn. We can't love you both. We don't want you either, anymore than you wanted yourself.

Orpheus, Condemned

If you could sing to Death all day,
charm it into stillness,
wouldn't you? Forever
in this victorious moment, young,
heroic, grateful
maiden at your side.

But to plead to remain
would cancel the glory, so you
trudge uphill, your feet
heavy as tombstones, your lyre,
a sack of coal dust in your arms.

You cast just one look of longing
at all you've lost, the way a prisoner
might try to memorize the sun
just before the heavy gates swing
shut—
    and they do swing shut, but
you're on the wrong side and she,
who would bear witness to your triumph,
is locked in Death's enchantment, weeping.

Your prize—to live,
fingers stiffening,
voice thinning.
Each morning your mouth fills with bile.
You sing the sun up
just so it can go down again.

The Wisdom of Solomon
after a painting by Giorgione

One woman kneels, her back to us,
a hand gesturing toward the baby
as if she'd like to get him off the cold, damp ground.
Another woman stands opposite, boldly facing the viewer,
her right arm pointed at Solomon as if to say,
Go on! Solomon has drawn a thin sword
and holds it up as though to scold the crowd.
He's the bearded figure, bareheaded, dressed in robes,
just realizing he's stuck. He vowed to slice a baby up
and suddenly the crowd got interested
sensing chaos, opportunity. He's a king.
He can't just bluster and go home.
He can't carve up a baby as if it were a pig.

His lifted arm is getting tired.
He wishes he'd slept late in silken sheets
or risen early to go hunting. He wishes
this baby had never been born. Even Solomon
knows a sword raised must be lowered.
But where? He feels the crowd
about to lunge when the kneeling woman
speaks: *Let her have the baby.* The moment
breaks like glass. The sharpened edges
of the crowd must cut someone,
but *later,* Solomon thinks, *later,* and tries
to smile as if he knew the outcome all along.

He takes the wet and squalling infant
and hands it to the stunned mother who has spoken.
Does he thank this quick-witted woman
who brought him back from disaster?
No, he scoops this victory up as if it were a grape,
beginning to think it his. The crowd

moves on, a withheld storm.
The opposing mother turns distraught.
But Solomon is happy.
He feels wise.

Lot's Daughter

Behold now, I have two daughters which have not known man; let me, I pray you, bring them out unto you, and do ye to them as is good in your eyes: only unto these men do nothing; for therefore came they under the shadow of my roof (Genesis 19:8).

Our father is old and there is not a man in the world to come into us after the manner of all the earth. Come, let us make our father drink wine, and we will lie with him, that we may preserve the seed of our father (Genesis 19:31-32).

The dark cave stank of wine and an old man's body.
Turning my face from the flickering torch,
I loosened my robe and placed my father's hands
on my breasts. He was insensible.
Did he think it was his wife, my mother
freed from brine, he groaned and turned from?
What could I do to rouse the only righteous man in
   Sodom?
Not stroke, not mouth, not my flesh moving over his,
not anything I'd heard the servants gossip of
or witnessed from my window in the rutted street below.
But then I whispered in his ear the story of his virtue,
how he'd tried to save the angels with his virgin
   daughters...
I forced myself to know what he would have permitted:
the men of Sodom strip his daughters,
bruising their breasts, pinching
their soft thighs, breaking
into that space between their legs
and then their buttocks.
I imagined being passed from hand to hand,
my sister screaming for father's help
while I kept a granite silence.

Meanwhile, I told him, inside the house the angels bless
you, are blessing, blessing, blessing you,
breaking the unleavened bread, their hands on yours,
eyes locked with yours, annointing your head,
and blessing you. Then he swelled
with pride and pleasure, hardened
and he took me.

First-born daughter, I passed him
to my sister as he would have passed me on.

Motherless in a world where regret
will harden you to salt, how shall we
care for Lot's seed?

Sudden Departure

Identification
Car keys
Cash
Address scrawled on back of a phone bill
Moon framed by the bedroom window
Cold light on the kitchen table
Change of clothes
Map

Somebody's sleep in your nostrils
Somebody's sweat in your mouth
Pinch of topsoil under your fingernails
Stone in your shoe
One bulb dormant in a dark pocket
Somebody's voice in your throat

Exile

While the difficult sun was courted
by the cobblestones below, she primed
her throat, a rusty pump, to purchase
bread and milk, then walked the city streets
as if their pavement were her lover.
She memorized the smell of every neighborhood:
burnt coffee, soot, lilac, curry, fish. What did it matter
that the writing on the wall couldn't spell
her name? Wind twisting like ribbons
through her hair. City on her skin.
Its bridges spanned her.

After the Visitation

Once you changed plugs on greasy engines.
Now you're canning peaches with the monks.

When the mountain filled your eyes like terror
you clasped the cold meat of your hands to pray.

You knew there'd be no rescue from inside this sun.
You eavesdrop on birds. Their song

translates into God's cold love. Years from now
children will still say, *This is where the Lady stood.*

The blue hem of her robe
scarring your eyes.

From now on your soul is dry ice
sizzling in someone else's service.

The Annunciation

In the waiting room, she's alone and thumbing
through the magazines—*Mothering, Baby Care*. In them,
   all women
are happy and well fed, babies shining
like light bulbs wrapped in gauze.
*Do I want to swell like her and have to rub
my swollen feet myself?* Few fathers in this magazine,
just doctors, and hints on making time for your husband
once the baby comes. Pictures of bright plastic beads,
mobiles, ads for the La Leche League,
a world she might step into.

They've tried to make this outer chamber cozy:
Cassatt's *Mother Bathing Child* on the wall, a choice
of herbal tea or a paper cup of cold spring water.
She saw the metal stirrups shining
through an open door on her way
to the cleanest bathroom she's ever used.
In her own, the plumbing's old and smells
of urine. She's handled shitty diapers in her life,
knuckles red from ammonia despite rubber gloves.
Live-in care for a colicky baby, she remembers
spit-up on her blouse, his small body like a separate world,
the tiny washcloth she used to bathe him, how he seemed
to smile as if she were his mother. When he turned two,
his parents got a nanny from an agency in London.
Now she works with a mask over her face,
testing pacemakers in a lab, content to return
to the one-room apartment filled with her own things.

The air conditioner is on too high. She shivers,
pulls her old blue sweater closer. She hears her name
called from another galaxy. A nurse

in blinding white comes toward her. *Mother of God,*
she begins, but she doesn't
know what to pray for.

Saint Joseph on a Roofing Job

Is that St. Joseph on our neighbor's roof
banging every morning? Graying hair tied back,
frayed denims, he must be worried
about his wild son who takes after
the mother's side of the family.
That boy and his gang of ragged friends stay up
all night. We hear them arguing
while they drink. In the morning,
Joseph has to step over large bodies
asleep in his living room. The police
have been there more than once.

Some days he starts his truck resentfully.
This morning he fits the shingles, nails
them neatly into place and thinks
of other girls he could have married,
of his friends whose boys are glad
to learn the family trade. His son can't hold
a hammer, prefers Mary's stories
to his jokes.

                    He tries
to be a good man, though he knows
he's inadequate to curb a son headed for destruction
or a mother in whose eyes the boy can do
no wrong. Sometimes it's got to be enough
to fix the leaking roof.

Death Salad

You made your bed, now lie in it, a strange saying, I claimed, since you usually make the bed after you're done lying in it. *No, you dress the bed,* my friend Carol told me. We mocked each other's accents—me from Long Island, she from Boston, both brought to the north Jersey suburbs for the good life. We read the same books over and over waiting for our breasts to grow and then her father died which made her strange to me. Did I seem cold? I was only ignorant and awed. She appeared touched by mystery, set apart. She'd become so tall and so good, taking her mother's arm each Sunday after Mass while the rest of us raced to our cars.

The day after Carol's father died, my mother sent me to visit, and I tasted the first really good potato salad of my life. It had olives in it and pickles. It taught me all the things a potato salad can hold. We liked that potato salad, Carol and I, but it was death salad brought over by neighbors because of her father. We sat in her living room and ate it together. Then we weren't best friends anymore.

Comfort Food

My dead friends materialize at the Holiday Inn breakfast
   buffet
to give me a message: *We're just invisible.*
That's what death means. They sit
at the table in Hawaiian shirts and Bermuda shorts
or plain dresses with jackets and sensible shoes.

What large appetites they have.
They keep bringing back eggs smothered
in Hollandaise, bacon and sausages,
muffins and toast, coffee rich
with cream, oatmeal sprinkled with brown sugar.
They eat with gusto, smacking their lips.
I'm so excited I can't touch a thing:
Wait till I tell Marie! Stephen, Linda Ruth! They nod
and keep chewing. They wipe the grease
off their chins, grin, give me a wink.
Then, one by one they disappear
sticking me with a check
enormous as grief.

Still, I'm not sad.
They'll be there, unseen, on the subway
reading the paper, swaying in time
with the train, or in the produce aisle,
boldly pinching the tomatoes,
lovingly squeezing each peach;
there, in the car that beats mine to the best parking space;
and in the sound of the wind—
their somnolent breathing
as they stand in the rain and stay dry.

Changeling

in memory of Catherine Young,
September 1949–August 2002

Deep within the grim woods of despair,
you swallowed all of terror's shining pills.
The kingdom of your body still sits here,

but you've been stolen. Empty eyed you stare
or weep. You smoke and mumble that you're evil:
twisted mantra, black wand of despair

which hypnotizes you, so we can't tear
it from your grasp or move the perverse will
that rules your body's kingdom sitting here.

You turned your head when I first ventured near:
"Don't try to rescue me," you said. I felt
impenetrable boundaries of despair.

We cannot find the charm to make you care—
not pills, not current coursing like a thrill
will animate your body that sits here,

head drooping like a broken bird's. Oh, steer
us from what's smug—the patronizing lilt,
the sideways glances masking our despair.
All we can give—this vigil. Sitting here.

March Thaw

The snow has mostly melted
leaving the lawn chairs bare
and covered with last autumn's leaves.
The earth half-roused, the bulbs
begin to push their green shoots through the ground.
You start to surface, too,
as if you'd had a long refreshing sleep,
your memory rolling back the stone
I placed before its tomb, your image
faint but taking color, more
spring-like than it ever was, here
among the crocuses and snowdrops.
I see you places you have never been:
propped against my neighbor's fence,
sitting at my picnic table drinking tea.
You seem at ease here in my yard
though others in my family do not see you.

Make your death real. Help me
resist this pastoral. Show me
all the pills you swallowed, the anti-freeze
you drank, let me touch
your sticky mouth and burning throat,
hold the dead weight of your body as it falls.

Meditation

"the little mind, your suffering ..." (from Stephen Levine's *Who Dies?*)

Let go,
though it's all that you have
the hurts you list over and over
your prayer, your importance.
Without them you might float
light as a balloon,
an inflated sphere
in a primary color, helpless
before any sharp branch or bird.
For a moment a child follows you
with her eyes, pointing with longing,
but soon she forgets, doesn't notice
your mind hung like tissue
from the tree, shreds
woven into some bird's nest.

Companion

I wake
then grief fills me
the way water fills the basin where I wash
or pours from the kettle into the cup.

All day I'm carried by its current.
I stretch toward those around me but cannot reach them.

From inside grief's caul I speak.
I do everything I need to do,
but my hands are clumsy inside grief's gloves.

Oh grief, you are so patient and persistent.
Everyday you come,
unwelcomed.
You stand close. You wrap your arms around me.
You whisper,
Don't worry.
I won't leave.

November Daybreak

The sky, dull lavender, night's fading
stain, bleaches to pewter
daybreak, becomes an indifferent suitor,
indifferently dressed, parading
quietly after trading
black velvet for something more muted,
more suited to morning's dignity. A hooded
sun. Some few clouds braiding
the horizon. One star
still out. One neighbor's light just on.
Geese heading south. Against the far
wall chrysanthemums brown
at their edges. Farther still, the charred
scent of leaves. A sense that things come round.

About the Author

Photo by Debi Milligan

Kathleen Aguero is the author of two previous volumes of poetry: *Thirsty Day* and *The Real Weather*. She has also co-edited two volumes of multicultural literature, *A Gift of Tongues* and *An Ear to the Ground*, and edited *Daily Fare: Essays from the Multicultural Experience*, for the University of Georgia Press. She lives with her family in Cambridge, Massachusetts, and is a Professor of English and Director of the College Composition Program at Pine Manor College.

Cedar Hill Books

DAUGHTER OF—*Kathleen Aguero*
$18—Poetry   ISBN: 1-891812-35-1

SET THIS BOOK ON FIRE!—*Jimmy Santiago Baca*
$15—Poetry ISBN: 1-891812-23-8

THE HEAT: *Steelworker Lives and Legends*
$15—Prose & Poetry ISBN: 1-891812-17-3

AMNESIA TANGO—*Alan Britt*
$10—Poetry ISBN: 1-891812-14-9

AMERICAN MINOTAUR—*Leonard J. Cirino*
$9—Poetry ISBN: 1-891812-22-X

96 SONNETS FACING CONVICTION—*Leonard J. Cirino*
$10—Poetry ISBN: 1-891812-20-3

THE TERRIBLE WILDERNESS OF SELF—*Leonard J. Cirino*
$10—Poetry ISBN:1-891812-00-9

THE JACKDAW POEMS—*Leonard J. Cirino*
$15—Poetry ISBN:1-891812-32-7

the despairs—*Cid Corman*
$15—Poetry ISBN: 1-891812-30-0

HANDFULS OF TIME—*Ruth Daigon*
$15—Poetry ISBN: 1-891812-36-X

INFINITIES—*Lucille Lang Day*
$15—Poetry ISBN: 1-891812-31-9

SUBURBAN LIGHT—*William Doreski*
$10—Poetry ISBN: 1-891812-16-5

ANOTHER ICE AGE—*William Doreski*
$15—Poetry ISBN: 1-891812-33-5

BODY AND SOUL—*Sharon Doubiago*
$15—Poetry ISBN: 1-891812-24-6

THE SILK AT HER THROAT—*James Doyle*
$10—Poetry ISBN: 1-891812-12-4

BLACK LIGHTNING—*Jean Flanagan*
$18—Poetry   ISBN: 1-891812-12-2

NEXT EXIT—*Taylor Graham*
$10—Poetry ISBN: 1-891812-13-0

NORMAL ENOUGH—*Yvette Hatrak*
$20—Fiction ISBN: 1-891812-34-3

BEYOND RENEWAL—*George Held*
$10—Poetry ISBN: 1-891812-29-7

WITHOUT PARADISE—*Richard Hoffman*
$15—Poetry ISBN: 1-891812-33-5

7th CIRCLE—*Maggie Jaffe*
$11—Poetry ISBN: 1-891812-07-6

THE PRISONS—*Maggie Jaffe*
$15—Poetry ISBN: 1-891812-21-1

SHADOW OF THE PLUM—*Carol Lem*
$15—Poetry ISBN: 1-891812-32-7

WHITHER AMERICAN POETRY—*Michael McIrvin*
$14—Critical Essays ISBN: 1-891812-26-2

THE BOOK OF ALLEGORY—*Michael McIrvin*
$10—Poetry ISBN:1-891812-03-3

OPTIMISM BLUES: Poems Selected & New—*Michael McIrvin*
$15—Poetry ISBN: 1-891812-37-8

PROVERBS FOR THE INITIATED—*Kenn Mitchell*
$11—Poetry ISBN: 1-891812-06-8

BRAMBLECROWN—*Georgette Perry*
$5—Poetry ISBN: 1-891812-25-4

GRAY AIR—*Christopher Presfield*
$8—Poetry ISBN: 1-891812-15-7

GUTTERSNIPE CANTICLE—*Amelia Raymond*
$9—Poetry ISBN: 1-891812-22-X

PARKING LOT MOOD SWING—*Doren Robbins*
$20—Prose Poetry   ISBN: 1-891812-11-4

"EDEN, OVER . . ."—*Tim Scannell*
$5—Poetry ISBN:1-891812-01-7

ROUTINE CONTAMINATIONS—*Deborah Small*
$24—Art / Prose ISBN: 1-891812-09-2

SOME SORT OF JOY—*John Taylor*
$15—Prose ISBN: 1-891812-08-4

THE WORLD AS IT IS—*John Taylor*
$15—Prose ISBN: 1-891812-04-1

KID WITH GRAY EYES—*Mark Terrill*
$10—Poetry ISBN: 1-891812-28-9

AMERIKA / AMERICA—*Marilyn Zuckerman*
$15—Poetry ISBN: 891812-40-8

PIECES OF EIGHT: *A Women's Anthology of Verse*
$10—Poetry ISBN: 1-891812-02-5

JAM: *Cedar Hill Anthology Series*
$10—Poetry ISBN: 1-891812-05-X